THIS JOURNAL BELONGS TO A VERY SPECIAL GIRL. THAT GIRL IS YOU!

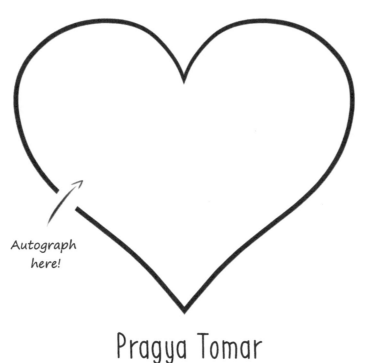

Autograph here!

Pragya Tomar

Cover Art by Giulia Iacopini

Inside art by Michela Fiori

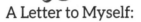

A Letter to Myself:

Today, I promise to love myself more than I did yesterday.

I'll prioritize my well-being and pursue my dreams with determination.

I'll take pride in my achievements, recognizing my brilliance.

My body is my home, my only place to truly live. I will treat it with care and kindness.

I am ready for the happiest, healthiest, wealthiest version of myself. I've worked hard for her.

I will give myself the love and care I'm so willing to give to others.

I love the effort I put in, the kindness I show, and how I handle challenges. I will value all those little things about myself that I often overlook. I am proud of the amazing person I'm becoming.

I don't have to be perfect. I don't have to be the best. I don't have to be flawless. The only thing I need is just to be myself.

When I can't control what's happening, I will control the way I respond to what's happening - for that is where my power is!

I admire my courage as I embrace a new phase of myself, knowing it will lead to positive growth and empowerment.

TABLE OF CONTENTS

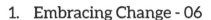

*For my loving daughter,
Nishka*

Change is the essence of life;
growth is the result of
embracing it with
courage and curiosity.

ISBN 978-1-952821-18-9 (Paperback)

https://www.PenMagicBooks.com

PenMagic Books provides special discounts when
purchased in larger volumes for premiums and promotional
purposes, as well as for fundraising and educational use.
Custom editions can also be created for special purposes.
In addition, supplemental teaching material can be
provided upon request.

Hey there, Awesome Girl!

Growing up can be like a roller coaster ride – full of twists, turns, and unexpected surprises. Imagine if you were on that ride without knowing anything about it - pretty scary, right? Well, life is a bit like that, especially when it comes to changes in our bodies, emotions, and all the stuff that comes with growing up.

I want to share a little story with you. My daughter went through the same wild ride not too long ago, and she felt a bit shy about asking questions. So, we sat down and had a heart-to-heart chat. I explained everything – from periods to growing up – in a way that made sense to her. And you know what? It made everything so much easier for her. Nothing was a surprise, and she could handle all the ups and downs like a pro.

Now, here's the thing. Some of her friends were struggling because they didn't have someone to talk to or didn't know what was going on. When my daughter saw this, she wanted to help. That's why I decided to write this book – to make sure every girl, no matter where she is or who she is, has a support system and her questions answered.

This book is like your guide to the roller coaster of growing up. We're diving into everything – changes in your body, staying clean and healthy, dealing with periods, understanding your changing emotions and feelings, and so much more. It's all about empowering yourself and being confident on this crazy, amazing journey.

So, buckle up, my awesome friends, because we're in this together, and I'm here to make sure you have the information you need to rock this ride called life!

Much love and appreciation,
Pragya Tomar

Remember

This journal is a private place to share your own unique reality; to explore, to be more aware of yourself, so write your ideas and opinions freely.

A GIRL'S COMING-OF-AGE IS A STORY OF TRANSFORMATION, FROM A BUD TO A BLOOM, EMBRACING HER UNIQUE BEAUTY AND INNER STRENGTH

Fill this
with your
favorite colors!

5

EMBRACING CHANGE

Hey Girl! Accepting change can be tough, especially when it involves our bodies growing and evolving. Embrace the idea that change is a part of life: Just like the seasons change and the weather shifts, our bodies change too. It's all a natural part of growing up. Knowing this can help us feel more at peace with the changes we're experiencing.

Instead of seeing change as something scary or unwelcome, try to approach it with curiosity and an open heart. Think of it as a new chapter in your life, full of exciting possibilities and adventures.

Even when change feels tough, there's usually a silver lining if we look for it. Maybe growing taller means you can reach things on the top shelf now, or your growing body means you'll look great in that outfit you've been eyeing. Finding the positives can help make change feel less daunting.

Change can be stressful, so it's important to take care of yourself during these times. Make sure to get plenty of rest, eat nourishing foods, and do things that make you feel happy and relaxed.

When change feels overwhelming, don't be afraid to reach out to friends, family, or other trusted adults for support. Talking about your feelings can help lighten the load and remind you that you're not alone.

Change takes time to get used to, so be gentle with yourself as you adjust. It's okay to feel a mix of emotions – just remember that you're doing the best you can, and that's enough.

Even when change feels hard, try to find moments of joy and gratitude along the way. Maybe it's noticing how much stronger you've become or celebrating small victories along the path of growth.

Remember, change is a natural part of life, and it's what helps us grow and become the amazing people we're meant to be. So embrace it with open arms and a hopeful heart, knowing that brighter days are ahead.

WHAT IS PUBERTY?

Hey there, Girl!

Let's talk about puberty in a simple way. Puberty is your body's way of getting ready for grown-up stuff, such as having babies. But hold on a sec! Just because your body is changing doesn't mean you're ready to be a mom yet. Puberty is all about your body growing and developing into an adult. It's stepping into a new phase of life.

But don't worry, it's not flipping a switch and suddenly you're all grown up. Nope, puberty takes its time, happening over a few years. So, while you might be noticing some changes already, such as your body shape shifting or your skin acting differently, just know it's all part of the journey. Your body's got your back, giving you plenty of time to adjust and embrace the amazing changes ahead!

Let me share a story about Sarah. 13 years old, Sarah was full of energy, and loved spending time with her friends. But lately, Sarah noticed some changes happening in her body. Her clothes felt tighter, her skin was breaking out, and she was feeling a little self-conscious.

At first, Sarah felt confused and maybe a bit scared. "What's happening to me?" she wondered. But then, she remembered something her mom had told her about puberty. "Puberty is a journey," her mom had said. "Your body is growing and changing, and that's perfectly normal."

Sarah decided to learn more about what was happening to her body. She read books, watched videos, and talked to her mom and older sister. She learned that puberty was a natural part of growing up and that everyone goes through it.

Armed with this new knowledge, Sarah began to see her body changes in a different light. Instead of feeling embarrassed about her acne or frustrated with her growing body, she started to embrace them as signs of her journey into womanhood.

Of course, there were still days when Sarah felt a little insecure. But whenever those feelings crept in, she reminded herself of all the amazing things her body was capable of. She celebrated her growth spurts, marveled at her changing shape, and even found joy in her newfound confidence.

Sarah also realized that she wasn't alone in this journey. She had friends who were going through similar experiences, and they supported each other every step of the way. They shared stories, laughed together, and offered words of encouragement when things felt tough.

As Sarah continued on her journey through puberty, she learned an important lesson: Change can be scary, but it can also be beautiful. By embracing her body changes with positivity and self-love, she discovered a newfound sense of strength and resilience. And with each passing day, Sarah grew more confident in herself and her ability to navigate the ups and downs of puberty.

So, dear girl, remember that you're not alone in your journey through puberty. Embrace the changes happening in your body, celebrate your uniqueness, and surround yourself with love and support. You're growing into a beautiful and strong young woman, and that's something to be proud of!

PUBERTY TIMELINES

AGE (YEARS)*

| 8 | 9 | 10 | 11 | 12 | 13 | 14 | 15 | 16 | 17 |

BUDDING BREASTS

GROWTH OF PUBIC HAIR

GROWTH SPURT BEGINS

FIRST PERIOD

GROWTH OF UNDERARM HAIR

CHANGE IN BODY SHAPE

ADULT BREAST SIZE

*Please be advised that the timelines provided are intended to offer a generalized understanding of the various stages of puberty development in girls and are not indicative of a standard framework. It is important to acknowledge that exceptions may exist.

Did you know that kids today are hitting puberty much earlier than their parents did? It's pretty mind-blowing! On average, they're starting to go through puberty about two years earlier than before. So, while your parents might have experienced those first hormonal changes when they were, say, 13 or 14, some kids today are starting to feel those changes at just 10 or 11 years old.

WHAT HAPPENS WHEN?

Let's chat about puberty timelines! Puberty usually kicks in around 9 to 10 years old and sticks around until you're about 16. But here's the thing: everyone's on their own schedule. Some start a little earlier, some a bit later. Your body's is working on it and it'll start when it's good and ready.

Now, onto the changes! Brace yourself for a mix of small adjustments and big transformations. Your body's like a superhero, knowing just what to do to help you grow up.

You might be wondering, "How much hair will I get?" or "What will my breasts look like?" Well, here's the thing: your body has its own plan for puberty. How fast things happen and what your body will look like in the end is a surprise only your body knows.

But guess what? Your body's got your back! It's working hard to help you grow into the awesome person you're meant to be.

Did you know that during puberty, both boys and girls experience growth spurts? This is when they grow rapidly in height and may experience changes in their body shape. These growth spurts are usually caused by hormones, particularly growth hormone and other hormones like testosterone and estrogen.

Hey girl, here's the scoop: each and every
one of us is totally awesome in our own unique
way. Whether you're into sports, art, science, or
just being you, remember that your awesomeness
shines bright, just like a star in the sky.

Puberty might change your body, but it won't
change the fact that you're amazing!

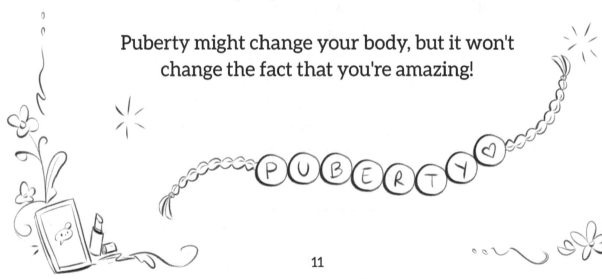

LET'S TALK ABOUT YOU!

Your name/age/grade:

Have you discussed puberty with a grown up?

Has your period started?

Are you experiencing changes in your body?

Is your hair growing in unexpected places?

Do you have body odor?:

Are you experiencing mood swings?

Do you know what PMS is?

Do you have oily skin and pimples on your face?

GIRLS' OUTER BODY CHANGES

Between the ages of 8 and 15, most girls will go through these changes:

Girls grow taller.

Bones in your face grow larger and longer causing your face to look less child-like.

Glands in your scalp produce more oil. Your hair may look and feel more oily.

Your skin may become more oily and you may get zits.

Hair grows under arms and on legs.

Breasts grow larger and fuller. They may feel tender or sore.

As sweat glands develop, you may notice increased sweating, which can lead to body odor.

Skin around the nipples gets darker in color. Nipples grow larger.

Waist may gets smaller.

Pubic hair grows around the genitals.

Hips broaden. Body begins to look more curvy.

Hands and feet grow rapidly.

Puberty Fact
The whitish fluid that may flow out of the vagina is normal and keeps it clean.

FACTS ABOUT PUBERTY

Hormones!
Girls produce more estrogen, which contributes to developments like breasts and menstruation. Boys produce more testosterone, leading to characteristics such as facial hair growth and a deeper voic

Growth spurt:
During puberty, you may experience a significant increase in height. Boys generally go through puberty later than girls, which can result in girls often appearing more mature than boys of the same age.

New changes:
You'll notice things like pubic hair, pimples , and may have some body odor —totally normal stuff!

Periods:
Yep, that time of the month. It starts during puberty and is part of how our bodies prepare for having babies one day.

Strong bones:
Puberty is important for building healthy bones. So, eat foods rich in calcium and stay active!

Feelings:
Hormones can make our emotions a roller coaster sometimes. Mood swings? Yep, they're real!

Brain boost:
Your brain is growing too, especially in areas like decision-making and handling emotions.

Remember, puberty is different for everyone, and it's all part of growing up. If you ever have questions or concerns, talking to a doctor can help!

YOU ARE NOT ALONE

Did you know you've got a massive squad of sisters all around the world? Yup, you're part of a crew of 1.2 billion girls between 0 and 14 years old! And guess what? They're ll diving into puberty just like you.

Think about it: right now, there's a girl somewhere across the globe going through some of the same stuff you are. Whether you're dealing with changes in your body or navigating those roller-coaster emotions, you're never alone in this journey.

So, even though our planet is huge, remember that you're part of this incredible sisterhood. Together, we're all in this wild ride called puberty, supporting each other every step of the way!

SELF-CHECK

Have you noticed any changes in your sleep
patterns or energy levels? _____
_____
_____

Are you experiencing any physical discomfort,
like cramps or headaches?_____
_____
_____

Have you noticed any mood swings or changes in your emotions?
_____
_____

Do you notice hair growth in your underarms and pubic area?
_____
_____

Are there any questions or concerns about puberty that
you'd like to talk about? _____
_____
_____

Are you feeling more self-conscious about your appearance?
_____
_____

Do you know how to use sanitary pads/tampons?_____
_____
_____

Are you experiencing any changes in your relationships with
friends or family members? _____
_____
_____

Our bodies are truly remarkable!

Our bodies possess an array of incredible abilities.

Our bodies are more than just things to admire; they're capable of so much.

Every body is unique, with its own form and
abilities. No body is identical, and all bodies are
worthy. Perfection doesn't exist in size,
ability, or color. Your differences make
you amazing, just as you are.

Start loving and accepting yourself just as
you are, right this moment. Don't delay
your journey to self-love—begin now, and
let it empower you.

PERIODS
AKA MENSTRUATION

Hey there, Girl!

Get ready, because your body's about to start producing some new fluids. Menstruation, aka getting your period, is a natural process where the lining of the uterus is shed through the vagina. For many girls, this is a big deal. Some cultures even celebrate it as a special milestone. But whether it feels super important or just like another part of life, it's all good.

Once your body starts developing breasts and pubic hair, it's a sign that your period might be on its way. Some girls get it as early as 9 or 10, while others might not start until they're 15 or 16.

You might hear a lot of talk at school about who got their period first, but remember, it's not a race. Whenever it happens for you, that's the perfect time. So, no need to stress about when it'll arrive. Your body knows when the time is right!

Your first period might be a few drops of blood in your undies, or it could be a bit heavier. The color can vary, too—bright red, dark red, even brownish. Everyone's body is different, so there's no one "right" way to have a period.

And hey, before or between periods, you might notice some clear or white fluid in your undies. That's called vaginal discharge, and it's totally normal. We'll dive deeper into that in the chapters ahead.

So, embrace the changes, girls! Your body's just doing its thing, and we're here to help you navigate every step of the way.

PERIOD PHASES

1 BLEEDING PHASE

1-7 DAYS

weaker immune system
lower energy levels
feeling tired
skin gets dry

HOW TO SUPPORT

rest days
ginger tea
dark chocolate
yin yoga
honor low energy
restore

Gentle exercise
Yoga or walking

2 FOLLICULAR PHASE

8-13 DAYS

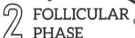

increased brain function
boost of energy
positive mood
skin is optimal

HOW TO SUPPORT

fermented foods
broccoli sprouts
citrus
vinyasa yoga
set goals
rising energy

Initiate new projects
Increased physical activity

3 OVULATORY PHASE

14-21 DAYS

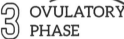

skin is at its best condition
feeling confident
less energetic

HOW TO SUPPORT

cardio
social
whole grains
higher energy
connect
eggs

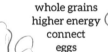

Lots of physical activity

4 LUTEAL PHASE

22-28 DAYS

sugar cravings
skin troubles
mood swings
anxiety, cramps

HOW TO SUPPORT

sweet potato
berries
strenght training
create
take action
leafy greens

Time for chores and taking care of your to-do lists

PERIOD POSITIVITY

Hey there, Awesome Girl!

When I first learned about periods, all I heard were negative things, and adults seemed shy to talk about them. That made me a little scared. You see, periods were a taboo topic. A taboo is something people try to avoid or feel uncomfortable talking about. Some even think periods carry a stigma, that they're something bad or unlucky.

But as I thought more about it, I realized I didn't have to feel that way. I didn't have to keep those negative feelings. So, I started talking openly about periods. I did fun activities and art projects that made me feel better, and I shared them with others. I called this being "period positive." It means understanding periods, talking openly about them, asking questions without fear, and not worrying too much about leaks or stains.

Talking About Menstruation

Sometimes, people feel uncomfortable talking about menstruation, so they use different words or talk quietly about it. These different words are called euphemisms. Euphemisms are used instead of more direct or sensitive words. For example, some people might call menstruation a "visitor" or "friend," or use phrases like "Aunt Flo" (like "flow," get it?). Others might joke about the color of their underwear, or use a secret code like "I got it."

But some euphemisms can reinforce old ideas about periods being dirty or dangerous, like calling it "the curse." Even the word "period" itself is a euphemism! It's short for "menstrual period." So, let's try to talk about menstruation openly and use the proper words without feeling embarrassed!

There's a lot of truth in the idea that giving something a name gives it power. Calling menstruation by its proper name— menstruation—is empowering! Talking openly about it makes it less scary. Plus, it sets an example and helps teach others about it. So, let's not be afraid to say the word "menstruation" and talk openly about it.

Feeling Ashamed of Periods

Periods can bring up lots of feelings, for both people who have them and those who don't. Sometimes, there's this feeling called shame. Shame can make you feel like you're doing something wrong, even if you're not. You might feel like people are avoiding you or avoiding talking about periods, which can make you feel uncomfortable. But feeling ashamed of periods isn't fair. It can lower your self-esteem and make you think there's something bad or wrong about you or your body, but that's not true. Don't be ashamed to talk about your periods. You have nothing to be ashamed of.

My Story

When I was almost 13, I was at a sleepover when I accidentally leaked menstrual blood onto my nightsuit. The other girls teased me about it, and I felt so embarrassed that I wanted to hide. But now, I want to help people worry less about leaks and focus more on breaking down the stigma around them. Period leaks happen, and it's nothing to be ashamed of. Let's change the way we talk about periods and make it okay to talk openly about these things!

YOU HAVE COMPANY

Learning About Periods and Puberty

Have you ever wondered how you first learned about periods and puberty? Lots of people learn from their friends, family, or even from movies or ads. But did the people you learned from seem confident and knowledgeable? And how comfortable do you feel talking about periods now?

Here are four stories of different girls experiencing their first period:

Emma's Story:
Emma was excited to become a teenager and felt like she was finally growing up. One day, while she was at school, she went to the bathroom and noticed some blood in her underwear. At first, she was confused and a little scared, but then she remembered what her mom had told her about periods. She realized it was her first period. Thankfully, she had been prepared and had some pads in her bag. She calmly used one and felt relieved. Emma also remembered to change her pad regularly throughout the day to stay comfortable and avoid any leaks. She felt proud to have reached this milestone and couldn't wait to tell her mom when she got home.

Sophia's Story:
Sophia was caught off guard when she got her period for the first time. She was at a sleepover with her friends when she felt something wet between her legs. Feeling embarrassed and unsure of what to do, she quietly excused herself to the bathroom and tried to clean herself up. While in the bathroom, she reached out to her friend's mother, who kindly helped her with cleaning up and provided pads to manage her period. When she got home, she confided in her mom about what had happened. Her mom reassured her and provided guidance on managing her period, including tips on using menstrual products and how to track her cycle for future reference. This support from both her friend's mother and her own mom helped Sophia feel more comfortable and prepared for the next time.

Aaliyah's Story:

Aaliyah had been eagerly awaiting her first period, but when it finally came, she was surprised by how much it hurt. She experienced cramps and felt uncomfortable for the first few days. Unsure of what to do, she confided in her older sister, who reassured her that it was normal to experience discomfort during menstruation and provided her with some tips for managing the pain, such as using heat packs and taking over-the-counter pain relief medication. Aaliyah felt relieved to know she wasn't alone in experiencing this and was grateful for her sister's support during this time.

Isabella's Story:

Isabella was terrified when she got her period for the first time. She didn't know what was happening and thought something was seriously wrong with her body. She kept it to herself, feeling scared and confused for days. Eventually, her mom noticed that something was bothering her and sat her down for a conversation about periods. Isabella felt relieved to have her mom's guidance and support. Her mom explained how to use pads and tampons, and she showed Isabella where they were kept in the house. She also reassured Isabella about common period symptoms like cramps and provided her with pain relief options, such as heat pads and over-the-counter medication. Isabella felt more prepared for managing her period in the future thanks to her mom's advice.

These stories illustrate the range of emotions and experiences that girls may have when they get their period for the first time. It's essential for girls to remember that they can always reach out to their parents or teachers for guidance when they experience something new or confusing, like getting their period for the first time. They are not alone, and there re caring adults who can provide support and information to help them through this transition.

PERIOD FACTS AND HACKS

Your first period is usually not that heavy. If you have no cramps, it's normal, every girl has a different body. Your second period can take more than a month or three to show up. Your body can take some time to regulate. Periods usually occur once a month. The menstrual cycle typically lasts around 28 days, but it can vary from person to person.

The average period lasts from three to seven days. Menstrual blood comprises the uterine lining, tissue, and blood. Variations in color, texture, and flow are normal throughout the menstrual cycle. Symptoms such as cramps, bloating, mood swings, and fatigue may accompany periods, but these can vary among individuals. Consult a doctor for personalized guidance and support.

Using pads, tampons, menstrual cups, or period underwear helps manage menstrual flow. Periods are a natural and healthy part of a girl's or woman's reproductive system, and they signal that the body is functioning as it should. Carry and keep your pads/tampons handy to use. Wear darker pants.

Drink plenty of water to lighten your period.
To ease cramps wear a heat pad.
Keep your body clean.
Change your pad every 2-3 hours.

Will I run out of blood?

You won't run out of blood during your period, don't worry! Some people get scared when they see a lot of blood because our brains are wired to protect us, and usually, bleeding means we've been hurt. But menstrual blood isn't like that—it's not a sign of injury. Instead, it's the lining that your uterus makes to create a cozy spot for a fertilized egg. So, when you see your period blood, remember that it's totally normal and nothing to be afraid of!

Cravings Before Your Period

Right before your period starts, you might crave foods that are sugary, salty, and fatty. But eating too much of these foods can make you feel tired and bloated. So, it's important to balance them out with plenty of vegetables, fruits, and water. Eating healthy helps keep your period regular.

Clots

Sometimes during your period, your menstrual blood can form clots, especially if you have a heavy flow. Clots are like thicker clumps of blood and are usually about the size of your fingertip. You might see one or more mixed in with your period blood, and they can look a bit like dark red or black jam or jelly. Seeing clots might be surprising, but they're usually nothing to worry about.

Stay Balanced

Excessive exercise and sudden changes in weight can mess with your period. So, it's important to try to stay balanced and take care of your body.

WHAT IS PMS?

Hey Girl, PMS stands for Pre-Menstrual Syndrome. It's like having some extra feelings and changes in your body before your period comes each month. Sometimes you might feel a little cranky, sad, or just not quite like yourself. Your body might also have some other signs, like bloating or cramps. It's all normal stuff, and it usually goes away once your period starts. Think of it like a little reminder that your body is getting ready for your period.

Managing emotions during PMS is all about finding ways to feel better when you're feeling a bit off. Here are some simple tips:

1. Talk About It: Share how you're feeling with someone you trust, like a parent, sibling, or friend. Sometimes just talking about it can make you feel a lot better.

2. Take Deep Breaths: When you're feeling stressed or upset, try taking slow, deep breaths. It can help calm your mind and body.

3. Do Something Fun: Take a break and do something you enjoy, like listening to music, drawing, or playing a game. It can distract you from negative feelings and boost your mood.

4. Get Moving: Exercise can help release feel-good chemicals in your brain, making you feel happier. Go for a walk, dance around your room, or play outside.

5. Practice Self-Care: Take care of yourself by getting enough sleep, eating healthy foods, and drinking plenty of water. It can make a big difference in how you feel.

My Story: You know, sometimes things aren't as simple as they seem. When I was a teen, I had trouble sleeping at night, and lots of other girls my age did too. It's called insomnia. So, even if someone tells you to just get enough sleep, it's not always easy to do. Especially because when you're in high school, there's a ton of homework to do, and some even have jobs and extracurricular activities. So, they end up sacrificing sleep to get everything done. It's definitely something important to keep in mind. Remember, it's okay to feel a little moody or emotional during PMS. Just be kind to yourself and try these tips to help you feel better.

People sometimes talk about "Coping with Periods" or "Dealing with Periods," but those words make it sound like having a period is a bad thing. That's why I like to think of it as "managing" because it means you're taking care of yourself. When you manage your period you are being kind to yourself and making decisions that help you feel proud and confident.

Talk to your friends and family about how you feel

Relax with a heating pad on your belly.

Write what you love

Try to get 7 to 8 hours of sleep each night.

Wear comfy and breathable clothes

If you suffer from cramps you may find certain hot teas help.

Eat fiber-rich food

Read good books

Change your pad or tampons frequently.

Enjoy a warm bath

Step into your room filled with your favorite soothing scent, bringing a sense of calmness.

Go for a walk for some fresh air

Avoid watching negative content because it can mess with your hormones and make you feel even more negative.

Reduce your screen time

Eat period friendly food

Do something that makes you happy

Listen to your favorite music

Try meditation or coloring this book!

Take a painkiller if necessary (ask an adult for advice first)

Find a period product that suits you

Drink water

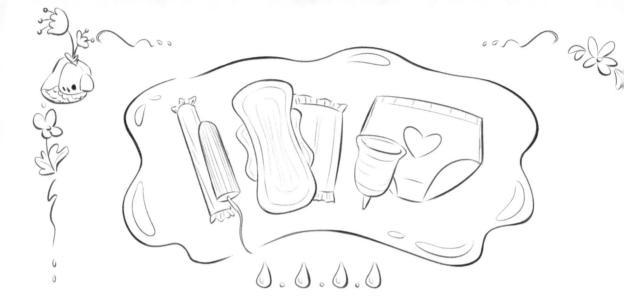

Pads, Tampons, and Other Period Products

The two most popular period products are pads (also known as sanitary napkins) and tampons. Both pads and tampons are made to absorb menstrual fluid. A pad is a rectangular piece of material that sticks to your underwear and collects the blood as it leaves your body. Tampons are slender cylinders of cotton and other materials designed to absorb the blood while it is still inside your vagina. Some companies also make menstrual cups, which are small plastic or rubber cups that catch the blood inside your vagina. There are girls who prefer pads, others who prefer tampons, and still others who only use cups. There are even women and girls who use all three during their period. It will take time and practice to figure out which one is best for you.

During the night, it's recommended to use a higher-absorbency sanitary pad or tampon to provide extended protection while sleeping. For sanitary pads, consider using an overnight pad designed to absorb more fluid and provide better coverage. Alternatively, menstrual cups can typically be worn for up to 12 hours, making them a convenient option for overnight use. It's essential to choose a product that suits your flow and comfort level and to change it as soon as you wake up in the morning to maintain hygiene.

All about Discharge

You know about the blood that comes out during your period, but there are other fluids involved in your cycle too. You might see them in your underwear or when you wipe after using the bathroom, and wonder what they are. These are different types of discharge – fluids made by your body's reproductive system.

The glands near the entrance to your vagina and urethra make a fluid to keep them moist and clean. Sometimes, your glands make another fluid that makes the walls of your vagina smooth and slippery. This happens when you feel attractive, excited, or aroused.

You might notice that the middle part of your underwear starts to fade or look bleached over time. That's totally okay and normal! Since vaginal fluid is a little acidic, it can cause this fading. It's nothing to worry about – there's nothing wrong with you or your underwear!

Your body always tries to keep a healthy balance of different bacteria inside you. But sometimes, if the balance gets messed up, you might have unhealthy discharge. This can happen if there's an infection caused by too much of the wrong bacteria. One possible cause is a yeast infection. They happen when the balance of bacteria in your vagina gets thrown off. This can be caused by using soap down there or wearing tight underwear. Yeast infections can make you itchy,

Another type of bacterial imbalance is bacterial vaginosis. It can cause gray, watery discharge that sometimes smells.

If you notice unhealthy discharge, like an unusual smell or color, it's important to take action. Two common causes could be bacterial infections or yeast infections. But whatever the cause, it's best to talk to your doctor to discuss treatment. They can provide guidance on how to manage it and ensure your health is taken care of properly.

HOW TO USE A SANITARY PAD

Using a sanitary pad is quite simple. Here's a simple guide to help you understand step by step:

1. Wash your hands: Before handling the pad, it's important to wash your hands with soap and water to keep everything clean.

2. Open the wrapper: Take the sanitary pad out of its wrapper. Be careful not to tear the pad while opening the package.

3. Remove the adhesive backing: Most sanitary pads have a strip of adhesive on the back that sticks to your underwear. Peel off the paper backing to expose the adhesive.

4. Position the pad: Place the pad in the center of your underwear, with the adhesive side facing down. Make sure the wider part of the pad is at the back and the narrower part is at the front.

5. Press down: Press down on the pad to make sure it sticks firmly to your underwear and stays in place.

Change regularly: It's important to change your pad every few hours, even if it's not completely soaked. This helps you stay clean and comfortable and reduces the risk of leaks and odors.

6. Dispose of used pads: When it's time to change your pad, carefully remove the used one and wrap it in toilet paper or the wrapper from the new pad. Then, throw it away in a trash can.

7. Wash your hands: After you've changed your pad, wash your hands again with soap and water to keep everything hygienic.

That's it! Using a sanitary pad is easy and helps you stay clean and comfortable during your period. If you have any questions or need help, don't hesitate to ask a trusted adult or an older sister or friend who has experience with pads.

MY PERIOD

1 remove sanitary pad

2 roll up sanitary pad

3 throw sanitary pad away

4 open new sanitary pad

5 put sanitary pad in underwear

6 take paper off wings

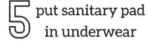

7 stick wings under

8 wash hands

9 you did it!

HOW TO USE A TAMPON

Using tampons for the first time can be a little intimidating, but with some guidance, it becomes much easier. Here are some things to keep in mind before using a tampon:

Read the instructions: Every box of tampons comes with instructions on how to use them. Before you start, take a moment to read these instructions carefully.

Choose the right size: Tampons come in different sizes and absorbencies. For your first time, it's best to start with a smaller size, like "lite" or "regular."

1. Relax: It's important to stay calm and relaxed when inserting a tampon. If you're feeling nervous, take a few deep breaths to help yourself relax.

2. Find a comfortable position: Some girls find it easier to insert a tampon while sitting on the toilet with their legs apart. Others prefer to stand with one leg lifted on the edge of the bathtub or toilet seat. Experiment to see what works best for you.

3. Insert the tampon correctly: Hold the tampon applicator firmly with your thumb and middle finger. Use your index finger to push the applicator gently into your vagina until your fingers touch your body. Then, use your thumb and middle finger to push the inner tube of the applicator, releasing the tampon into your vagina.

4. Don't rush: Take your time when inserting the tampon. It may take a few tries to get it right, and that's okay. If you're having trouble, don't hesitate to ask for help from an adult or older sibling.

5. Change regularly: Tampons need to be changed every 4-8 hours, depending on your flow. Remember to remove the tampon before inserting a new one.

6. Stay relaxed during removal: To remove the tampon, gently pull on the string until it slides out. If you're having trouble, relax your muscles and try again. Never leave a tampon in for more than 8 hours.

7. Disposal: Wrap the used tampon in toilet paper and dispose of it in the trash. Do not flush tampons down the toilet, as they can cause blockages.

Stay confident: Remember, using tampons is a normal part of growing up, and many girls use them without any problems. If you have any questions or concerns, don't hesitate to talk to a trusted adult or healthcare provider.

PERIOD UNDERWEAR

You know, period underwear has really changed things up for how you handle your periods. They can hold a lot of blood, like around two pads' worth, which means you don't have to worry about leaks anymore, which is such a relief. And guess what? There are even bathing suits made for periods now! It's amazing how they've thought of everything. Also, you might consider using menstrual cups—they're eco-friendly and super convenient.

HOW TO USE A MENSTRUAL CUP

1. WASH

2. FOLD

3. INSERT
IN

4. RELAX

8-10 hours

5. PUNCH & PULL OUT
OUT

6. WASH

Menstrual cups might not work for everyone, but they offer a convenient and eco-friendly option for many. Made of silicone, these cups can collect menstrual blood for 8 to 10 hours before needing to be emptied, rinsed, and reinserted. As long as there's access to clean water, you can reuse them for years, making them a sustainable choice for managing your periods.

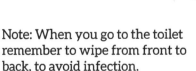

Note: When you go to the toilet remember to wipe from front to back, to avoid infection.

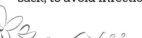

ASK FOR HELP

Hey there, Girl,
It's important not to feel ashamed to talk to someone you trust about any concerns you have. Whether it's a friend, family member, or a trusted adult in your community. Reaching out for help is a brave and smart thing to do. Grown-ups, especially, can offer advice and support because they've been through similar experiences themselves. If you're ever unsure or need help, don't hesitate to ask a grown-up to take you to a doctor or offer guidance. You're not alone, and there's always someone ready to help.

I get a lot of pain every month at the same time during my cycle. What should I do?

"How can I support you?"

I am 14, my periods have not started yet. All my friend's have. I am concerned.

"Thank you so much for telling me."

My periods are so heavy, I don't know how to manage it. Can you please help?

I always get really depressed, anxious, and angry right before my period and it's affecting my life. What's wrong with me?

"Can I do anything to help you?"

With 12 months in a year, you might be expecting 12 cycles per year too. The reality is, you could have anywhere from 11 to 16 full cycles, depending on how long your cycle is. The dates don't exactly line up once per month.

	J	F	M	A	M	J	J	A	S	O	N	D
1												
2												
3												
4												
5												
6												
7												
8												
9												
10												
11												
12												
13												
14												
15												
16												
17												
18												
19												
20												
21												
22												
23												
24												
25												
26												
27												
28												
29												
30												
31												

SYMPTOMS KEY

	SPOTTING
	LIGHT
	MEDIUM
	HEAVY
	ACNE
	CRAMPS
	CRAVINGS
	FATIGUE
	HEADACHE

CYCLE LENGTH

JANUARY	
FEBRUARY	
MARCH	
APRIL	
MAY	
JUNE	
JULY	
AUGUST	
SEPTEMBER	
OCTOBER	
NOVEMBER	
DECEMBER	

NOTES

_____
_____
_____
_____
_____
_____
_____
_____
_____

REMEMBER THIS ...

I embrace the changes happening in my body with grace and confidence.

I will not hesitate to ask for help.

I trust in my body's natural growth and transformation during puberty.

I welcome each stage of puberty as a beautiful part of my journey to womanhood.

I am resilient and capable of navigating the changes puberty brings.

I am grateful for every experience and lesson.

Hi!

I believe in myself.

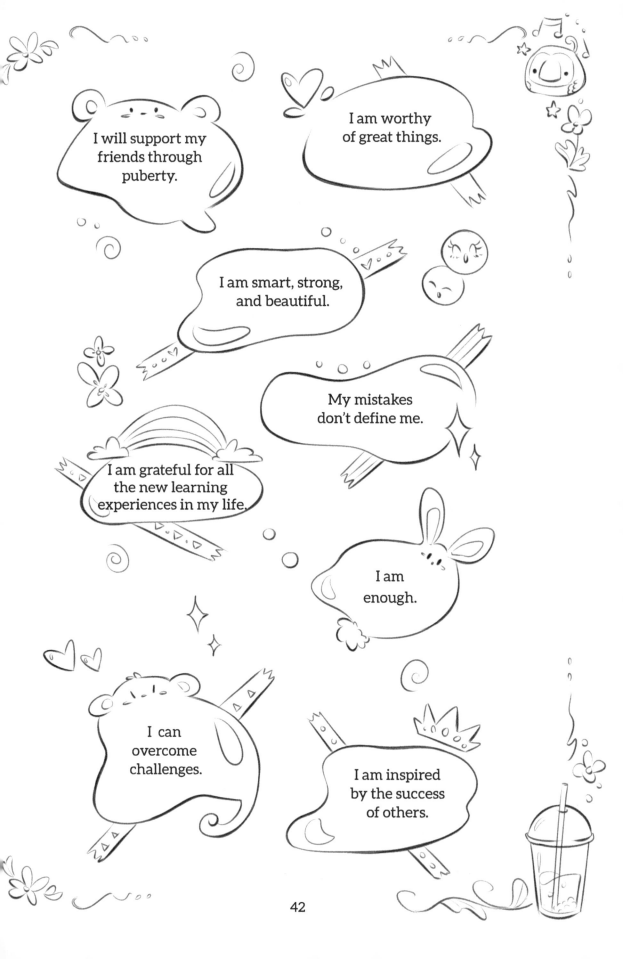

I will support my friends through puberty.

I am worthy of great things.

I am smart, strong, and beautiful.

My mistakes don't define me.

I am grateful for all the new learning experiences in my life.

I am enough.

I can overcome challenges.

I am inspired by the success of others.

BREASTS & BRAS

Now I am a young woman

This is a good thing!

My body is changing

I used to be a small girl

My breasts are growing

I'm growing taller

An adult will help me find a bra that fits and will teach me how it works

Soon, I may need to wear a bra

It's ok to ask questions

Most women, and big girls wear bras

A bra will cover my breasts and, hold them in place

Growing up is an adventure full of surprises!

If my bra no longer fits, I can tell an adult

I will need new bras as my body grows

Fifty percent of women have one breast that is smaller than the other. The left one is usually the smaller one and doctors are not sure why.

Stage 1	
Stage 2	
Stage 3	
Stage 4	
Stage 5	

Hey there, Amazing Girl,

Welcome to the exciting part of puberty when your breasts start to develop! It's a journey that takes several years, but whenever it happens, it's a big change. I'll make sure you have all the info you need to feel confident and powerful as your body grows and changes.

Whether you're excited about getting your first bra or feeling a bit nervous, it's important that it feels comfy and reflects who you are. Did you know that not every girl needs to wear a bra? Lots of girls and women don't wear them at all! Bras are meant to help when you're moving a lot, like running or playing sports. You might not need one until your breasts start feeling a bit bouncy or if they feel tender under your clothes. And guess what? It's totally okay if you don't want to wear a bra! Sometimes we feel pressured to wear one because of what we see on TV or what our friends are doing. But if it doesn't feel right for you, that's okay. Just talk to a grown-up you trust if you're thinking about getting one.

BREASTS AND BRAS

Hey Girl,

So, when you start growing up, one of the first things you might notice is that your chest starts to change. That's when you might see little bumps called 'budding breasts' starting to appear. Sometimes, as they grow, they might feel a bit tender or sore. That's totally normal and just means they're getting bigger.

To help with the tenderness and support your growing breasts, you might want to try wearing a training bra. These are like soft, comfy tops that gently hold your breasts in place. They come in all sorts of colors and designs, kind of like crop tops!

It's important to know that everyone's breasts are different. They can be big or small, and nipples can be all kinds of colors. And guess what? You can't rush them to grow faster or change their size. They're unique to you and grow at their own pace.

Oh, and don't worry if your nipples look a bit different too, like if they're inverted (which means they point inward). That's totally normal too! Just remember, your body is doing its own thing, and it's all part of growing up.

Lots of women have gone through the experience of growing breasts and getting their first bra. For some girls, it's a really cool moment. For others, it's no big deal or even a bit annoying. And you know what? That's totally okay! Let me share some stories from women who have been through it before you:

Samantha's Story: Samantha was excited to get her first bra. She felt like it was a rite of passage and couldn't wait to pick out something cute. When she finally tried it on, she felt a little strange at first, but soon got used to the feeling. She loved how it made her feel more grown-up and confident.

Emily's Story: Emily wasn't too thrilled about getting her first bra. She felt self-conscious about her changing body and didn't want to draw attention to herself. When she tried on her bra for the first time, she felt awkward and uncomfortable. It took some time for her to get used to wearing it, but eventually, she realized it wasn't as big of a deal as she'd thought.

Lily's Story: Lily was indifferent about getting her first bra. She didn't see what all the fuss was about and just wanted something comfortable to wear. When she tried on her bra, she was surprised by how different it felt, but she quickly adjusted to it. She appreciated the extra support it provided and was glad to have it for when she needed it.

Aisha's Story: Aisha was nervous about getting her first bra. She felt like it was a sign that she was growing up and wasn't sure if she was ready for that. When she tried on her bra, she felt a mix of emotions—excitement, nervousness, and a little sadness that she was leaving her childhood behind. But as she looked in the mirror, she felt proud of the young woman she was becoming.

These stories show that everyone's experience with getting their first bra is different, and that's perfectly okay!

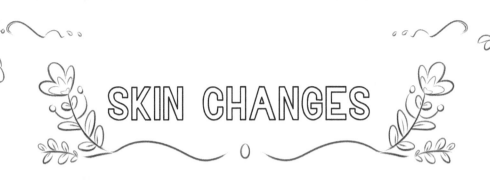

SKIN CHANGES

Did you know that your skin is like a big blanket that covers your whole body? Yep, from your head down to your toes! During puberty, your skin might need some extra love and care to keep it healthy and glowing. But don't worry, it's not too complicated. All you need to do is drink water, get enough rest, and eat good food.

Now, let's talk about something that many girls worry about during puberty: pimples and blackheads. Puberty doesn't mean you're stuck with acne forever. When your body starts making more hormones, it also produces extra oil. This oil can mix with sweat and dirt and clog your pores (little holes in your skin), leading to acne and blackheads.

But here's the good news: having a simple skincare routine can help keep breakouts under control. Just wash your face every day with a gentle cleanser and use a moisturizer afterward to keep your skin hydrated. If you're dealing with more stubborn breakouts, you can ask a trusted adult to help you pick out some anti-acne cream from the store. Look for one that's oil-free and soap-free—it's better for your skin.

Sometimes, though, acne can be tricky to manage on your own. If you're struggling with really tough breakouts that won't go away, it might be a good idea to see a dermatologist, which is a doctor who specializes in skin. They can give you stronger medicine to help clear up your skin and get you feeling confident again.

SOME THOUGHTS ON MY SKIN

If you feel good with foundation, wear it. Or don't. That's okay too.

Your complexion doesn't have to be perfect for it to be glowing

Some companies really profit on you hating your skin. Take back the power by loving yourself!

Instagram filters don't actually show you what skin looks like in real life—be careful about comparison

Acne is normal, not gross

Skin is never perfect and that's okay!

Your worth doesn't come from the flawlessness of your skin

PERSONAL HYGIENE TIPS FOR TEENS

Hey there, Strong Girl!

Personal hygiene is super important for all of us because it helps us stay healthy and feel good about ourselves. When we wash our hands regularly, brush our teeth, and take showers, we can avoid getting sick and feeling yucky. Plus, keeping clean makes us feel more confident and comfortable around other people. When we smell fresh and look neat, it's easier to make friends and feel accepted in social situations. Taking care of our skin is also a big deal. By washing our face and moisturizing, we can prevent pimples and other skin problems that can be embarrassing. And let's not forget about body odor! With all the changes happening to our bodies during adolescence, we might sweat more and start to notice some smells. But if we use deodorant and change our clothes and bathe regularly, we can keep that under control.

Good personal hygiene is crucial for teens because it:

1. Keeps you healthy by preventing the spread of germs and reducing the risk of illnesses like colds and infections.

2. Boosts self-esteem and confidence, helping you feel better about yourself and more comfortable around others.

3. Promotes social acceptance and respect, leading to positive perceptions from peers and fewer instances of bullying.

4. Improves your appearance, making a positive impression in various situations such as school, job interviews, and social gatherings.

5. Prevents skin problems like acne.

6. Controls body odor.

Toilet hygiene:
Ensure to wipe your genitals after using the toilet and wash them while bathing.

Skincare:
Keep your skin clean with mild soap or cleansers to reduce the risk of skin problems such as acne and blackheads.

Oral care:
Brush and floss at least twice daily to prevent bad breath and tooth decay.

Bathing:
Bathe regularly to avoid developing body odor and sweat stains. In case of profuse sweating an antiperspirant/deodorant may help control sweat production.

Hands:
Wash your hands really well every time you go to the bathroom, and before lunch. Trim your nails.

SOAP

Feet:
Wash your feet and change your socks daily.

Clothes and shoes:
Avoid wearing clothes or shoes that have absorbed sweat. Always opt for clean ones to prevent smelly feet and body odor.

Menstrual hygiene:
Follow the doctor's instructions on the frequency of changing your sanitary napkins or tampons and how to use them correctly.

Hair:
Brush your hair daily. Avoid wearing it loose to school to reduce the risk of lice. Wash your hair as necessary, to remove grease and dandruff.

3 hours

YOUR PHYSICAL AND MENTAL HEALTH

Hey there, Lovely Girl!

So, you know how sometimes you feel a bit stressed out or worried about things? Well, regular exercise can actually help with that!

When you move your body, like when you play sports, go for a run, or even just take a walk, it sends special signals to your brain. These signals release chemicals called endorphins, which are like your brain's own little mood boosters. They make you feel happy and relaxed.

Regular exercise also helps improve your sleep, which is super important for your mood and how you feel during the day. When you sleep well, you wake up feeling refreshed and ready to take on whatever comes your way.

Plus, exercising can give you a break from schoolwork or other stuff that might be stressing you out. It's like hitting the reset button for your brain!

So, whether you're shooting hoops, dancing around your room, or going for a bike ride, remember that exercise isn't just good for your body—it's great for your mind too!

Regular physical exercise is like giving your body and mind a super boost! Just like how eating healthy food makes your body strong, exercising does too, but in a different way. When you move your body by running, jumping, or playing sports, it helps make your muscles and bones stronger. Plus, it keeps your heart healthy, like a superhero protecting your body.

So, remember, regular exercise isn't just about keeping your body fit, it's about keeping your mind happy too!

BENEFITS OF EXERCISE ON MENTAL HEALTH

Sharper memory and concentration

Endorphins help you concentrate and feel mentally sharp. It simulates growth of new brain cells and keeps your brain active.

Better sleep

Exercise helps regulate your sleep patterns.

Increased self-esteem

In addition to making you look better, committing to an exercise routine can increase your sense of self-worth.

More energy

Every time you get your heart rate up with exercise, you give your body a much needed jolt.

Stronger resilience

Exercise teaches you to manage stress in a healthier way.

Note: There's much more to mental health than getting enough exercise, and some kids and adults face serious issues, particularly during the middle school years. It's important to be aware that not all mental issues can be fixed by exercise and sleep, as this can be dangerous for teens who don't seek help for serious depression and anxiety.

BEST FOODS FOR YOUR BODY

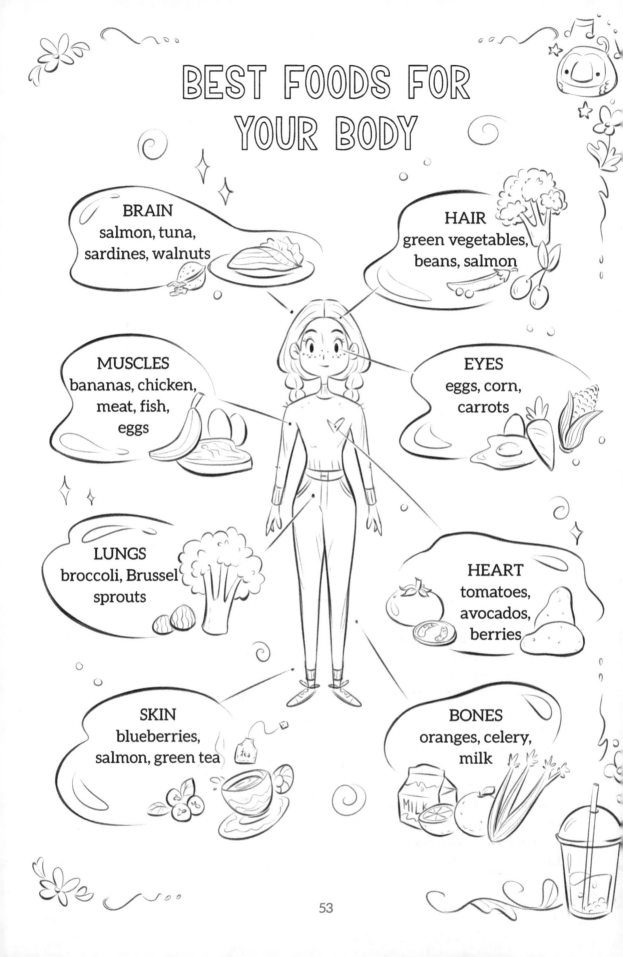

BRAIN
salmon, tuna, sardines, walnuts

HAIR
green vegetables, beans, salmon

MUSCLES
bananas, chicken, meat, fish, eggs

EYES
eggs, corn, carrots

LUNGS
broccoli, Brussel sprouts

HEART
tomatoes, avocados, berries

SKIN
blueberries, salmon, green tea

BONES
oranges, celery, milk

ANIKA'S STORY

14-year-old Anika loved spending time outdoors, playing sports, and hanging out with her friends. She enjoyed eating snacks like chips, cookies, and soda while watching TV or playing video games. But one day, Anika started feeling sluggish and tired all the time. She noticed that her skin wasn't as clear as it used to be, and she was having trouble concentrating in school.

At first, Anika didn't think much of it. She figured it was just stress from school or maybe she wasn't getting enough sleep. But as the days went by and she didn't feel any better, Anika started to worry. She knew that feeling tired and unfocused wasn't normal, and she wanted to figure out what was going on.

So, Anika decided to take responsibility for her health and make some changes to her diet. Instead of reaching for chips and cookies, she started snacking on fruits, vegetables, and nuts. She swapped out soda for water and herbal tea. She also made an effort to eat balanced meals with plenty of lean proteins, whole grains, and colorful vegetables.

At first, it was hard for Anika to resist the temptation of her favorite snacks. But as she started to see and feel the benefits of her healthy choices, it became easier. She noticed that she had more energy throughout the day, her skin started to clear up, and she was able to focus better in school.

Anika's friends were impressed by her dedication to making healthy choices, and some of them even joined her in making changes to their own diets. Together, they discovered new healthy recipes and found fun ways to stay active.

As time went on, Anika continued to prioritize her health and well-being. She learned that being responsible for her choices could have a big impact on how she felt and how she lived her life. And she lived happily and healthily ever after.

FEEL
HELP
SEE
TRY
ENJOY

color this!

56

LET'S UNDERSTAND OUR MAGICAL BODY!

Hey there, Smart Girl! Let's chat about how babies are made and what reproduction is all about. During puberty, our bodies start changing to get ready for something super special: having babies when we're grown-ups. Reproduction is all about how we may become parents and start our own families some day.

Alright, let's dive into the main players in reproduction: the vagina, ovaries, fallopian tubes, and uterus. Think of them as a superhero team working together to make babies happen! The ovaries are like small factories producing eggs that could become babies. The fallopian tubes act as tunnels, carrying these eggs to the uterus, which is like a comfy home where a baby can grow. And when the time comes, the vagina acts as the door for the baby

So, reproduction is all about how our bodies can create new life and make families. It's pretty amazing, right? If you have any questions, feel free to ask your doctor or a grown up.

DID YOU KNOW?

All the eggs in your ovaries have been there since you were born? They've been waiting their turn to one day be fertilized and become a baby or to get their special invitation to the period party.

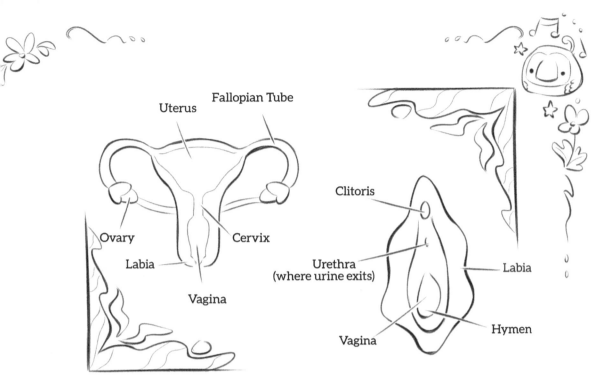

The vagina is like a special tunnel inside a girl's body. It has a few important jobs:

Periods: Every month, the uterus (where a baby grows) gets ready for a baby. If there's no baby, the lining of the uterus comes out through the vagina, and that's what you see during your period.

Babies: When someone has a baby, the baby comes out through the vagina. It stretches to let the baby through, kind of like a tunnel opening up.

Pee: The vagina doesn't have a job with pee, but right above it, there's a tiny hole called the urethra. That's where pee comes out from the bladder.

LOVE YOUR BODY!

"How you love yourself is how you teach others to love you." - Rupi Kaur

Hey Girl! When you love yourself, your soul lights up! You are a magnet to those who love, respect, and appreciate your energy. Everything begins with how you feel about yourself. You should eat like you love yourself. Move like you love yourself. Speak like you love yourself. Act like you love yourself. Loving yourself starts with respecting yourself, which starts with thinking of yourself in encouraging ways. You, as much as anybody else, deserve your love and kindness. Inspire yourself, have faith in yourself, and love yourself. Never doubt who you are. Spend time exploring who you are. In the end, the only person you're ever going to truly live with is yourself.

To begin loving yourself start saying these affirmations out loud.

- I willingly embrace myself as I am in this moment, with love and acceptance.
- I deeply value the unique beauty that defines me.
- I regularly express gratitude for all the blessings in my life.
- I have confidence in my capacity to care for myself, while also being open to seeking assistance when necessary.
- I refrain from self-criticism.
- I refrain from criticizing others.
- I grant myself forgiveness when I make mistakes.
- I extend kindness to others while honoring my own needs.
- I hold myself accountable for my choices and actions.
- I commit to loving myself to the fullest extent possible.

If you notice a little voice in your head saying mean things about your body, remember to be kind to yourself. Tell that little voice, "MY BODY IS STRONG. MY BODY CAN DO AMAZING THINGS. MY BODY IS MY OWN."

Try to write your own self-care list. What activities or thoughts make you feel calm? What makes you happy? Keep your list somewhere close and use it wherever you feel you need it.

Start a journal. Each day, write down how you felt that day. If you had negative thoughts, write down how you dealt with them. If you had positive thoughts write down how they made you feel. If you enjoy art, try drawing, painting, or collaging in your journal.

Write down some of the things that you like to do and explain how your body helps you to do them. When you're finding it hard to love your body, read over your list and you will remember all the reasons why your body is worth loving.

When you hear your friends saying something negative about their bodies, gently remind them of the lessons you have learned from this book. You can lift your friends up by listing all the things you love about their personalities or by celebrating the amazing things their bodies can do.

If you're experiencing negative thoughts, start a conversation with someone you trust. It's important to share how you are feeling with others. Reaching out and seeking help is incredibly brave.

YOUR BODY IS UNIQUE

No one has a body quite like yours, and that's amazing!

Every body is different, and every body is a good body.

Puberty is a time when your body changes and grows on the inside and outside to look more like an adult's body.

12 WAYS TO LOVE YOURSELF

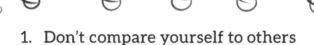

1. Don't compare yourself to others

2. Take good care of your body

3. Stand up for yourself

4. Forgive yourself

5. Support yourself

6. Be honest with yourself

7. Give yourself a treat

8. Say "NO" when you need to

9.. Believe in your abilities

10. Appreciate your life

11. Treat youself with kindness and respect

12. Explore and pursue your passions
    with enthusiasm!

If you are ever finding it hard to love your body, try writing a list of all the great things that your body helps you to do. Here are some example:

I love that my ears can hear music and that my body can dance to the sound.

I love that my body is strong enough to pick up my little sister and give her a big hug.

I love that my hands help me to create beautiful things.

I love that my nose can smell the saltiness of the sea and the flowers in the garden.

I love that my eyes can see my favorite TV show and read my favorite book.

Write or draw the things you love
about your body in the hearts below!

I love...

I love

I love

I love

I love

I love

I love

BODY IMAGE

How do you feel about your body? _____

_____

_____

_____

_____

Why do you think you feel this way?

_____

_____

_____

_____

Are there any aspects of your appearance that you feel
insecure about? _____

_____

_____

_____

_____

How do you think social media affects your body image?

_____

_____

_____

_____

Do you compare your body to others'? If so, how does that
make you feel? _____

_____

_____

_____

BODY IMAGE

How do you handle negative comments or judgments about your appearance? _____

_____

_____

_____

What roles do your friends play in shaping your body image?

_____

_____

_____

_____

Have you ever felt pressured to look a certain way? _____

_____

_____

_____

_____

What strategies do you use to feel confident and comfortable in your own skin? _____

_____

_____

_____

How do you think your body image affects your overall self-esteem?

_____

_____

_____

_____

DORY'S STORY

14-year-old Dory loved to dance. She had been taking ballet class-es since she was little and dreamed of one day becoming a profes-sional dancer. Dory worked hard in her dance classes, practicing every day and pushing herself to be the best dancer she could be.

But one day, Dory overheard some girls in her dance class whis-pering and giggling while they looked at her. She couldn't hear everything they were saying, but she caught snippets of words like "chubby" and "big." Dory felt a sinking feeling in her stomach as she realized they were talking about her body.

Dory had always been self-conscious about her body. She wasn't as tall or as slim as some of the other girls in her class, and she sometimes felt like she didn't belong. But she loved to dance, and it made her feel confident and alive.

As the whispers and giggles continued, Dory started to feel ashamed of her body. She began to doubt herself and her abilities as a dancer. She started skipping meals and exercising excessively, hoping to change her body to fit in with the other girls.
But no matter how hard she tried, Dory couldn't change the shape of her body. She felt like she was failing as a dancer and as a person. She started to lose her passion for dance and began to avoid going to class altogether.

One day, Dory's dance teacher noticed that she wasn't her usual self. She pulled Dory aside and asked her what was wrong. Dory hesitated at first, but then she opened up about how she had been feeling. She told her teacher about the whispers and giggles and how they had made her feel ashamed of her body.

Her teacher listened quietly, then she took Dory's hands and looked her in the eyes. She told Dory that she was a beautiful and talented dancer, and that her body was strong and capable. She reminded Dory that dance was about expressing yourself and telling stories through movement, not about conforming to a certain body type.

Dory's teacher helped her see that body shaming was hurtful and unnecessary, and that Dory didn't need to change anything about herself to be worthy of love and respect. Dory realized that she had been letting other people's opinions define her worth, and she decided to embrace her body and her passion for dance.

From that day on, Dory danced with confidence and joy. She surrounded herself with people who supported and uplifted her, and she never let anyone else's words bring her down again. Dory learned that true beauty comes from within, and that she was perfect just the way she was. And she lived happily and authentically ever after.

Draw a picture of yourself in your favorite costume

TELL ME MORE

What is the best compliment you've ever received?

What do you see when you look in the mirror?

How do you think other people see you?

SELF-CHECK

How would you describe your confidence levels in different areas of your life, like school, friendships, or hobbies?

_____

_____

_____

What are some things you like about yourself?

_____

_____

_____

_____

Do you ever compare yourself to others? If so, how does it make you feel? _____

_____

_____

_____

_____

What accomplishments are you proud of?

_____

_____

_____

_____

How do you handle setbacks or failures? _____

_____

_____

_____

_____

SELF-CHECK

Do you feel comfortable expressing your opinions and
standing up for yourself? _____

_____

_____

_____

Are there any activities or hobbies that make you feel good
about yourself? _____

_____

_____

_____

How do you talk to yourself when you make a mistake or
face a challenge? _____

_____

_____

_____

Have you ever felt pressure to change something about
yourself to fit in or meet others' expectations? _____

_____

_____

_____

Who are the people in your life who make you feel
supported and valued? _____

_____

_____

_____

_____

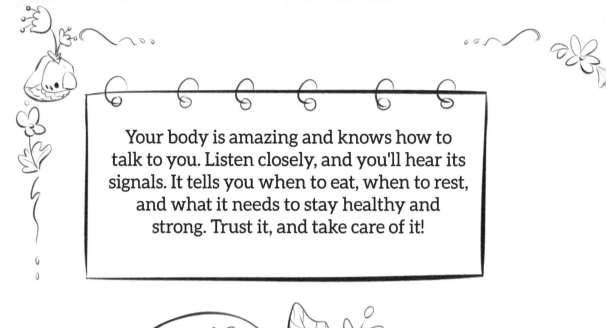

Your body is amazing and knows how to talk to you. Listen closely, and you'll hear its signals. It tells you when to eat, when to rest, and what it needs to stay healthy and strong. Trust it, and take care of it!

Listening to your body is key to self-care. It's like having your own personal guide telling you what it needs to feel good and stay healthy. Trust yourself and take care of your body!

Sometimes your body might not cooperate with what you want to do, and it can feel frustrating. But remember, your body is on your team, even when it feels like it's not. Keep going, and give yourself the love and care you need. You've got this!

When you're feeling down about your body, remember it's doing its best. Every body is unique, with its own strengths. Find those strengths, embrace them, and love yourself for who you are. You're amazing just the way you are!

If you didn't like the last list, here are more things to try when you're feeling down. Taking care of your mind and body is called "self-care." It's a great way to be kind to yourself and a skill you can use your whole life.

1
Stand before the mirror and say, "I am strong. I am capable."

2
Go outside and enjoy nature. Sit under a peaceful tree or lie on the grass, feeling the blades against your skin. It helps you connect with nature.

3
Write down three things you are truly grateful for.

4
Wear a crazy and colorful outfit and confidently strut around until you begin to genuinely feel that confidence radiating from within!

5
Blast your favorite music at full volume and dance wildly just for the sheer joy of it! You'll soon notice a smile spreading across your face, and you won't be able to contain it.

6
Help a friend or family member in need. Stepping out of your own thoughts to support others can bring a sense of relief and fulfillment. Engaging in acts of kindness will leave you with a warm and positive feeling knowing you've made a difference in someone else's life.

7
Explore activities like knitting, crocheting, cross-stitching, or drawing patterns. Engaging in these creative pursuits can provide a calming experience as you focus your attention on using your hands and concentrating on one task at a time.

8
Take some time for slow stretching in a peaceful environment; this can help you feel more connected and comfortable in your own body. If you're interested, you could also explore yoga.

9
Experiment with taking photos of objects around your home. Viewing life through the lens of a camera can offer a fresh perspective and ignite your creativity.

10
Explore positive quotes until you discover one that resonates with you deeply. Write it down or print it out and carry it with you. When you're feeling low, take a moment to read it and find comfort in its uplifting message.

BEING AUTHENTIC

"Be who you are and say what you feel because those who mind don't matter and those who matter don't mind" - Bernard M. Baruch

Hey Girl! Authenticity is when you say and do things you actually believe. It is to know who you are and being brave enough to accept it and live it.

When you stop pretending to be anything other than who you truly are, and instead, put all of that energy into being yourself, your life will transform. You won't have to worry about fitting in, because you will be focused on simply being YOU! When you stop pretending to be anyone else, you will become your truest self and who you were meant to be.

Authenticity is a practice - a conscious choice of how we choose to live. It's about being honest with your choice, the choice to let our true selves be seen.

Hey Girl! Try being authentic... be completely yourself so that everyone else feels safe to be themselves too.

AUTHENTIC

Self-exploratory questions

What
is it that you are
passionate about?

What things
make you happy
to be alive?

How
are you making the
world a better place?

I
wish I knew
more about...

When I grow
up I want to...

Something
I want to invent to
make life better...

HEALTHY BOUNDARIES

I don't allow people to treat me that way.

That's not something that I want you to know about me.

You are making me feel uncomfortable. Can you please stop?

You're standing too close. Can you please back up?

I don't think that's funny at all. Please stop.

I need you to respect what I said or else, I'll need to leave.

I decide how much personal information I share with others.

I say no to things that don't feel safe to me..

Instead of trying to fit in, I express myself authentically.

That is something that I don't want to talk about.

I respect the opinions of others while also having my own.

I prioritize time to nurture my goals and well-being.

I only share my personal space and energy with those I trust.

I don't feel guilty about needing space or a break.

Speaking up when someone speaks down to me is important.

I don't like being called that name.

SETTING BOUNDARIES

A boundary is a rule you set about how you want to be treated by others. It's all about letting people know what's okay and what's not okay. You have the right to set boundaries about anything that makes you feel uncomfortable or could hurt you. Here are some things you can say when others are crossing your boundaries.

When someone is doing something that makes you feel uncomfortable or crosses a line, it's important to speak up and let them know. Use clear and direct language to explain how their actions are affecting you. Don't be afraid to express yourself honestly and assertively.

Your boundaries are important, and you have the right to stick to them. Don't let anyone pressure you into changing your mind or make you feel guilty for setting boundaries. If something doesn't feel right to you, it's okay to say no and stand firm in your decision. Your feelings matter, and you deserve to be respected.

Use I statements.
"I feel uncomfortable when you..."

If someone keeps ignoring your rules, maybe they're not being a good friend. Real friends always respect each other's boundaries and make sure everyone feels safe and comfortable.

CONSENT

Hey there Girl, Thanks for hanging in there. Now I would like to talk about something very important. It's called CONSENT.

Consent means saying "yes" freely and happily when you're okay with something. It's like playing a game – you and the other person both need to agree on the rules. For example, if someone wants to give you a hug, and you're okay with it, that's giving consent. But if you don't want a hug or feel uncomfortable, it's important to say "no," and that's okay too.

Boundaries: Boundaries are like your personal space rules. They help you feel safe and comfortable. For instance, you might decide that only your doctor can touch your private parts for medical checkups. It's important to let people know about your boundaries and to respect other people's boundaries too. If someone makes you feel weird or uncomfortable, it's okay to say "no" and tell a trusted adult, like your parents or a teacher.

Remember, your feelings matter, and it's important to speak up if something doesn't feel right. And yes, always share what's happening with your parents or teachers – they're there to help and protect you.

- Don't meet strangers alone, especially if you feel uncomfortable or unsure.
- No one should touch your private parts except your doctor for medical reasons only.
- If you're not comfortable, don't meet with adults who make you feel uneasy.
- Learn to say "NO" if something feels wrong or makes you feel unsafe.
- Don't accept gifts or favors from strangers, especially if it doesn't feel right.
- If something awkward or strange happens at school, don't keep it to yourself – tell your parents or a teacher right away.

Remember, your safety and comfort come first, so always trust your instincts and speak up if something doesn't feel right.

You have a right to like hugs and kisses...or not. It's the same for everyone else.

Your body belongs to you. Nobody should touch it in ways that you don't like.

If the other person doesn't say yes, don't hug them. They may be too shy to say no. They might think it will hurt your feelings or make you angry. It doesn't mean they want a hug.

Respect their response, whether it's a yes or a no. Understand that consent can be revoked at any time, even if it was initially given.

It's the same for kisses, snuggles, holding hands and this rule also applies to grownups. Adults shouldn't hug you or kiss you without your consent, either.

Feel like hugging someone? Ask them first. If the other person says no, don't give them a hug.

BEING RESPONSIBLE

Hey there, Awesome Girl!

When you hear the word "responsibility," what do you think of? Maybe it's finishing your schoolwork on time or lending a hand with chores at home. It could also mean keeping an eye on your younger sibling.

Responsibility includes all of those things, but it's also about something deeper. It's about looking inside yourself and doing your best to be a great person. It's about finding ways to help others too. In simple words, when you're responsible, you're taking steps to make your life the best it can be.

As we grow up, we gain more control over our lives. We can decide what we do and who we spend time with. It's exciting because we're in charge of our actions, responsibilities, and health choices. But with this power comes responsibility.

Every choice we make has an outcome. When we make good choices, we feel proud of ourselves and the results. But if we make bad choices, we have to face the consequences. It's up to us to create the life we want.

When we consistently make good choices, we earn trust from adults. This trust brings more freedom and opportunities. However, if we keep making bad choices, we risk losing the freedom we enjoy.

Remember, making healthy decisions isn't just about avoiding trouble or pleasing adults. It's about taking care of ourselves and our future. We have the power to shape our lives, starting with the choices we make.

Let me tell you a story about a girl named Alexa who learned the true meaning of responsibility.

> Hey, you know that big, never-ending thing called the Internet? Well, whatever you post on it stays there forever. Social media can be pretty cool. You can chat with friends, check out what everyone's up to, and share funny pics. But, it's not all fun and games. Be careful what you post because it's out there for anyone to see, even your parents or teachers. And there are some sketchy people out there too. Don't give out personal info or accept friend requests from strangers. If someone online gives you a bad vibe, trust your gut and tell an adult right away.

ALEXA'S STORY

16 year old Alexa loved spending time with friends, playing video games, and exploring the neighborhood park. But as Alexa grew older, she started to realize that with more freedom came more responsibility.

One day, Alexa's parents decided to go out on a Saturday night, leaving Alexa home alone for the first time. At first, Alexa was thrilled at the idea of having the house to herself. She imagined staying up late, ordering pizza, and having friends over for a movie marathon.

But as the weekend approached, Alexa's parents sat her down for a serious talk. They reminded Alexa of the importance of being responsible while they were away. They went over the household chores that needed to be done, like taking out the trash, feeding the pets, and keeping the house tidy. They also emphasized the importance of staying safe, locking the doors, and not inviting strangers over.

At first, Alexa felt a bit overwhelmed by all the responsibilities. They worried about forgetting to do something important or making a mistake. But then, she realized that being responsible meant taking care of herself and her home. It meant making smart choices and thinking about the consequences of her actions.

So, when the weekend arrived, Alexa rose to the challenge. She made a checklist of chores and stuck to a schedule to ensure everything got done. She resisted the temptation to stay up too late or invite friends over without permission. Instead, she enjoyed her independence responsibly, knowing that she were proving herself trustworthy in the eyes of her parents.

When Alexa's parents returned home, they were impressed by how well Alexa had handled everything. They praised Alexa for her maturity and responsible behavior. And as Alexa reflected on the weekend, she realized that being responsible wasn't just about following rules— it was about taking pride in doing the right thing, even when no one was watching.

LET'S TALK ABOUT YOU!

Do you make your bed in the morning?

_____

Do you tidy up after yourself, putting things back where they belong?

_____

Do you manage your time well, completing homework and tasks on time?

_____

Do you respect others' belongings and personal space?

_____

Do you apologize and take responsibility when you make a mistake?

_____

Do you communicate openly and honestly with your friends and family?

_____

Do you stand up for what is right, even if it's difficult?

_____

Do you listen to others without interrupting?

_____

Do you follow rules and guidelines at home and at school?

_____

Do you prioritize your well-being, including getting enough
sleep and exercise?

_____

Do you show kindness and empathy towards others?

_____

Do you handle your emotions in a healthy way, seeking help if needed?

_____

Do you contribute positively to your community or school?

_____

Do you take care of your belongings, keeping them clean and organized?

_____

RESPONSIBLE CITIZENS

I take care of the environment.

I follow the law.

I volunteer and help my community.

I'm always ready to assist my parents with chores.

I treat others with respect.

I am learning about people from other lands

I work hard to improve.

I make sure to be tidy and put things away after using them.

I volunteer my time to help those in need.

I tell the truth and take responsibility for my actions instead of blaming others.

I save water, gas, and electricity whenever possible. I switch off appliances when they're not in use.

I respect other people's time.

I try to save some of my pocket money and avoid being wasteful with money.

I am polite and considerate to other people, especially my elders.

I stay informed about local and national issues.

I never litter; I either take it home or use bins. I make an effort to recycle waste like paper and glass.

I treat school's and other people's property with respect.

I make sure to be kind to others and willing to help people in need. I am kind to animals.

MY HOUSEHOLD RESPONSIBILITIES

Color your every-day chores

Put dishes in dishwasher

Set the table

Walk the dog

Vacuum the floor

Tidy the bedroom

Wash the dishes

Make your bed

Water the plants

Wipe down surfaces

Put away clean clothes

Clean the fridge

Keep your room organized

Do the ironing

Clear the table

Clean the kitchen

Dust the furniture

Do the laundry

Help with cooking

Help with shopping

Feed the pet

Organize your closet

Sweep the floor

change the sheets

Scrub the floor

Clean the bathroom

Take out the trash

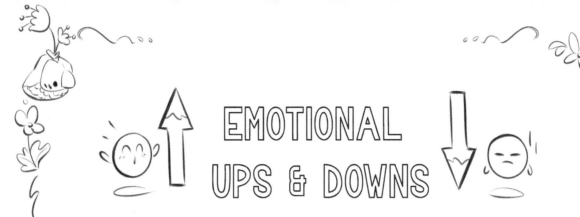

EMOTIONAL UPS & DOWNS

Hey there, Girl!

Puberty can sometimes feel like a wild roller coaster ride, with its ups and downs that can leave you feeling like you're on a whirlwind adventure. Have you ever felt like storming off to your room because of something your mom said? Or maybe you've noticed that your feelings seem to change faster than the weather? Well, guess what? It's all part of growing up, and hormones play a big role in this crazy journey.

Yep, those hormones we've been talking about are at work once more! As your body grows and changes, it starts releasing new chemicals that can make your emotions feel a bit unpredictable. So, if you ever feel like your emotions are all over the place, just know that it's completely normal—and you can chalk it up to those pesky hormones!

Feeling all sorts of emotions is a big part of being human. From happiness to sadness, from excitement to fear, our feelings make us who we are. And guess what? During puberty, it's our emotions get turned up to full blast! Yep, those new hormones swirling around inside us can make our feelings feel bigger and more intense than ever before.

Sometimes, you might find yourself crying for reasons you can't even explain. Other times, you might feel really angry about things that used to just bother you a little. And hey, that's totally normal. Puberty is a time of big changes, both physically and emotionally. You might even start feeling new emotions, like jealousy or maybe even have a crush on someone.

But here's the thing: no matter what feelings you're experiencing, it's important to remember that you're awesome just the way you are. Your feelings might feel overwhelming at times, but they won't last forever. So take a deep breath, hold on tight, and remember that it's all just part of the journey called puberty.

Emotional self-awareness is the ability to identify and understand your emotions and how they affect your behavior. Sensations and feelings are like waves in the ocean. Some come crashing in, while others roll in gently, but they always come and go. We can't stop the waves from coming, but we can be aware of their presence, so they don't knock us over. Inner peace begins the moment you choose not to allow anything outside of you to disrupt your emotions.

Accept your feelings without judgment. Remind yourself, you are not your emotions. Say this to yourself, silently or (when possible) aloud: "I can handle this emotion. **I am strong and able to handle this wisely, easily, calmly."**

EMOTIONAL MANAGEMENT

How do you usually handle big emotions like anger or sadness?

_____

_____

_____

Have you noticed any changes in your emotions lately?

_____

_____

_____

What activities or strategies do you find helpful for managing stress?

_____

_____

_____

Are there any situations or triggers that make you feel
overwhelmed? _____

_____

_____

_____

How do you cope with peer pressure or difficult social situations?

_____

_____

_____

Do you have someone you feel comfortable talking to when
you're feeling upset? _____

_____

_____

_____

Do you recognize when you need a break to recharge?
What activities help you recharge?

_____
_____
_____
_____
_____

Can you describe a situation where you found it challenging to
express your emotions in a healthy way?

_____
_____
_____
_____
_____

List any mindfulness or relaxation techniques that
you've found helpful?

_____
_____
_____
_____
_____

How do you make sure to take care of yourself and your
mental health?

_____
_____
_____
_____
_____

HOW TO BECOME EMOTIONALLY MATURE

Accept your emotions. Don't deny them. Acknowledge and accept that they are there.

Understand and acknowledge your feelings and why you have them.

Let go of your need to control your emotions.

Let emotions exist without judgment.

Identify and label your emotions To stay mindful, say to yourself, "this is anger" or "this is anxiety".

Use coping skills that help you deal with your emotions instead of ignoring them.

Learn how to identify what you are feeling.

Allow yourself to feel whatever emotions come up without judging them as good or bad.

Inquire and investigate. Ask yourself, "What triggered me? Why do I feel this way?"

Be willing to be vulnerable and share your struggles.

Face your emotions with acceptance. Notice the emotions and where you feel them in your body.

Try to put yourself in someone else's shoes.

Know that your feelings won't last forever.

Ask for help when you need it.

Own up to your actions instead of blaming others when things don't go as planned.

Even when an emotion feels overwhelming, remember that it will pass.

Learn to apologize when you make a mistake.

Learn how to set healthy boundaries.

MY FEELINGS

Color the feelings on this
page according to the chart.

COLOR	I FEEL THIS WAY...
green	Often
blue	Sometimes
yellow	Never/Hardly Ever

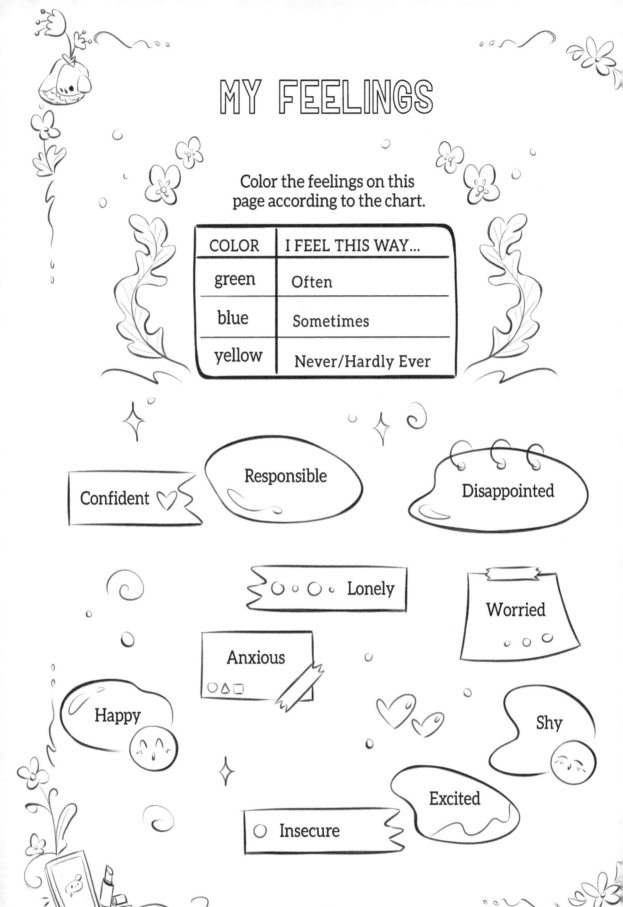

Confident

Responsible

Disappointed

Lonely

Worried

Anxious

Happy

Shy

Excited

Insecure

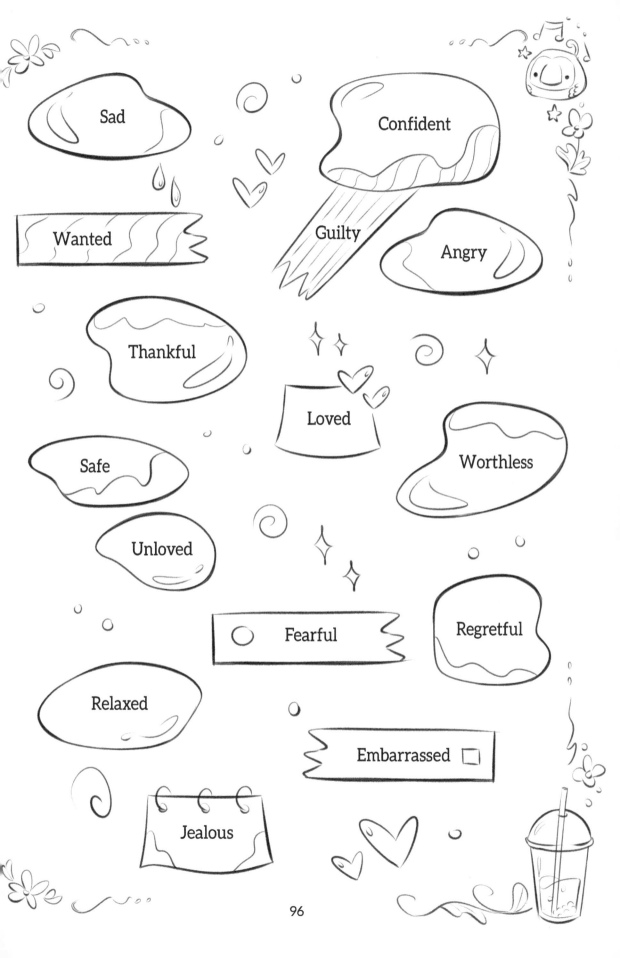

Sad

Confident

Wanted

Guilty

Angry

Thankful

Loved

Safe

Worthless

Unloved

Fearful

Regretful

Relaxed

Embarrassed ☐

Jealous

DEALING WITH FEELING EMBARASSED

Embarrassment is the feeling you get when you do something that might cause others to laugh or make fun of you. It often makes you feel awkward or uncomfortable.

LAUGH IT OFF

In embarrassing moments, finding humor in the situation can be helpful. Laughing along with others can make it feel less awkward, especially for harmless mishaps like spilling juice or dropping your belongings. This coping skill can ease tension and help you move past the embarrassment more easily.

IT HAPPENS TO EVERYONE!

Keep in mind that everyone has experienced embarrassment at some point in their lives. You're not alone in this. When you're feeling embarrassed, talking to friends and family members and hearing their stories about similar experiences can be comforting and reassuring.

MOVE ON!

When embarrassing things happen, it's natural to keep replaying the moment in our heads. But dwelling on it isn't helpful and only makes us feel worse. Instead, try to let go of what happened. The sooner you move on, the sooner others will too. Remember, you have many positive qualities. Focus on your strengths rather than on the embarrassing moment.

LEARN FROM IT

Usually, when we feel uncomfortable emotions, like embarrassment, there's a chance to learn and grow. Are there steps you can take to prevent feeling embarrassed in similar situations in the future? For instance, if you felt embarrassed because of a mistake during a piano recital, you could commit to practicing more regularly.

30 DAYS OF AFFIRMATIONS

- Every day is a new day
- I am capable
- I am worthy
- Nothing lasts forever
- My past does not define me

- I can handle it
- I will honor my needs
- I will not compare myself to others
- I can heal
- I will focus on what I can control

- I will let go of perfection
- I am safe
- I am thankful
- I am allowed to rest
- I deserve good things

- Someone loves me
- I trust myself
- I am always enough
- I deserve to be cared for
- I will be okay

- Every breath calms me
- I can say no
- I am brave
- I believe in myself
- There is good all around me

- I can move at my own pace
- My vibes are good
- I will receive love
- I can find joy
- I can do my best

COPING SKILLS

Ride a bike or skateboard

Ask for help

Play with toys

Kick, bounce, or throw a ball

Explore or discover nature

Cook or bake

Eat healthy

Practice gratitude

Take good care of the earth

Smile and laugh

It's okay to cry sometimes.

Take a shower or bath

Use kind and compassionate self-talk

Listen to music

Play a board game

Color, paint, draw

Write a journal

Make a collage

Drink a warm cup of tea

Take slow, mindful breaths

Cuddle or play with your pet

Practice relaxation techniques

Drink water

Clean, declutter

Garden or do yardwork

Read a book

Create origami

Get a hug

Play outside

Do a puzzle

WHAT MAKES A GOOD FRIEND?

Dear Girl,

Friends are like the pillars of our lives, supporting us through thick and thin. We naturally seek companionship because it's part of who we are. Having good friends and being a good friend yourself is super important. While there's no rulebook for friendship, it's not as mysterious as it seems. Being a good friend means being the kind of friend you'd want for yourself. But what exactly makes someone a good friend?

Friendships are like treasures, aren't they? You might have a best friend who knows all your secrets and loves hanging out with you. You share laughs, maybe even cry together sometimes, and forgive each other when things go wrong.

But here's the thing: not all friendships last forever. Some might stick around for years, while others might only last a few weeks or months. And as you grow up and change, your friendships might change too. It's normal for things to shift, just like the seasons.

You know, being a good friend is really important. But sometimes, even if you try your best, someone might not want to be your friend anymore. Imagine having a best friend since kindergarten, and then one day, they just don't want to be your best friend anymore. It can feel really sad. But it's okay. It doesn't mean they're bad or that something's wrong with you. It just means you're both growing up and changing. And as we change, what we look for in a friend might change too. When we get older, we start to like different things and have new hobbies. So, it's normal to find new friends who like the same things we do. That's just part of growing up.

WHAT IS A TRUE FRIEND?

REAL FRIEND	FAKE FRIEND
Like you for who you are and makes you feel good about yourself	Likes only parts of who you really are and makes you feel bad about yourself
Cheers you on and wants you to win, too	Cheers you on when you're not playing against them
Includes you and makes sure there's room for you to sit or join the game	Excludes you or doesn't think to include you or make room for you
Good friends don't have rules about how or when you can hang out with them.	Makes you do something or give them something before you can play
Asks what you want to do or play	Will play with you only if you do what they want to do
Does not treat you differently when other kids are around	Treats you diffently or ignores you when others are around
Apologizes when they hurt your feelings.	Don't realize when they hurt your feelings
Wants to be with you and spend time with you	Wants to be with you when it's convenient for them or they're lonely
You feel comfortable to be yourself around them	You change who you are, what you wear, or how you talk to fit in with them
Listens to you when you tell them to stop doing what they're doing	Does not listen to you when you'll tell them to stop doing what they're doing
Stands up for you even when you're not there to defend yourself	Makes fun of you behind your back or let others make fun of you
You feel great after you've spent time with them	You feel upset or kinda weird after you've spent time with them

SOPHIE'S STORY

Sophie and Lily had been friends since they were kids. They did everything together, from playing on the playground to sharing secrets. Sophie always felt happy and supported when she was with Lily.

As they got older, Sophie noticed some changes in their friendship. Lily started making fun of Sophie's interests and hobbies, calling them "weird" or "lame." Sometimes Lily would exclude Sophie from group activities or ignore her texts for days.

At first, Sophie brushed off these behaviors, thinking they were just part of growing up. But deep down, she felt hurt and confused. She didn't understand why Lily was acting this way or what she had done wrong.

Sophie decided to talk to her older sister, Mia, about her concerns. Mia listened carefully and explained that true friends should lift each other up, not tear each other down. She encouraged Sophie to reflect on her friendship with Lily and consider whether it was healthy for her.

After much thought, Sophie realized that her friendship with Lily was taking a toll on her self-esteem and happiness. She knew she deserved better treatment from her friends. With a heavy heart, Sophie decided to distance herself from Lily and seek out friendships that were supportive and uplifting.

As Sophie began to distance herself from Lily, she discovered new friendships with peers who shared her interests and values. These friends listened to her, respected her boundaries, and made her feel valued and appreciated. Sophie realized that healthy friendships should make her feel happy, confident, and supported.

Though it was difficult at first, Sophie soon felt a sense of relief and freedom from toxic relationships. She focused on nurturing her new friendships and building connections with people who brought out the best in her. With each passing day, Sophie grew stronger, wiser, and more confident in her ability to choose healthy friendships.

Sophie's journey taught her valuable lessons about the importance of surrounding herself with positive influences and setting boundaries in her relationships. As she entered high school, Sophie felt empowered to choose friends who celebrated her for who she was and supported her growth and happiness.

This story highlights the importance of recognizing the signs of unhealthy friendships and making choices that prioritize one's well-being and self-respect. It encourages readers to value themselves and seek out friendships that bring out the best in them.

PEER PRESSURE

Hey Girl! Let's discuss peer pressure, an essential aspect of our growth and development. Peer pressure is the influence that peers, or people in your age group, can have on you to adopt certain behaviors, attitudes, or values in order to fit in or be accepted by the group. It can come in many forms, ranging from subtle suggestions to direct pressure to engage in specific actions or behaviors.

For example, imagine a group of friends who regularly go to parties where violent video games are played. If one friend in the group decides not to play because they don't feel comfortable with it or because it makes them anxious, they may feel pressure from the other friends to join in. This pressure could be overt, such as teasing or peer encouragement, or it could be more subtle, like feeling left out or excluded from the group if they don't participate.

Peer pressure can also manifest in other ways, such as pressuring someone to try cigarettes, drugs, or alcohol, engage in risky behavior, or even skip class. It's important to note that peer pressure can be both positive and negative. Positive peer pressure encourages behaviors that are beneficial or healthy, such as studying hard for exams or participating in sports. Negative peer pressure, on the other hand, promotes behaviors that are harmful or risky, such as smoking, drinking alcohol, or skipping

Ultimately, peer pressure can be a powerful force, especially during adolescence when the desire to belong and be accepted by peers is strong. Learning to navigate peer pressure and make decisions that align with your own values and beliefs is an important part of growing up and developing independence.

"Be yourself; everyone else is already taken." - Oscar Wilde

ALICIA'S STORY

17 year old, Alicia had always been known as the "goody two-shoes" in her friends group. She always followed school rules and made sure to finish her homework on time. But things in her high school started to change.

Her friends began experimenting with alcohol and cigarettes, and suddenly Alicia found herself feeling left out. They would invite her to parties where everyone was drinking, and she felt the pressure to join in.

At first, Alicia resisted. She knew that drinking was against her values and that it could have serious consequences. But as the invitations kept coming and her friends started teasing her for being "too uptight," Alicia began to doubt herself.

One night, Alicia decided to go to a party with her friends. She told herself that she would just have one drink to fit in. But as the night went on, Alicia found herself drinking more and more, trying to keep up with her friends.

The next morning, Alicia woke up with a pounding headache and a feeling of regret. She knew that she had let herself down and that she had given in to peer pressure.

From that day on, Alicia decided to stay true to herself no matter what. She realized that her true friends would accept her for who she was, and that she didn't need to change herself to fit in. And although it wasn't always easy, Alicia learned to say no to peer pressure and to stand up for what she believed in.

PEER-PRESSURE

Can you share a time when you felt pressured by your friends to do something you weren't comfortable with?_____

_____

_____

_____

_____

What are some examples of peer pressure you've experienced or witnessed? _____

_____

_____

_____

_____

How do you usually respond when you feel pressured by your peers? _____

_____

_____

_____

_____

How do you think peer pressure affects different aspects of your life, such as school, social activities, or personal choices? _____

_____

_____

_____

Describe specific situations or environments where you feel more susceptible to peer pressure? _____

_____

_____

_____

How do you distinguish between positive peer influence and negative peer pressure?

_____

_____

_____

_____

Have you ever stood up to peer pressure? If so, how did you handle the situation?

_____

_____

_____

_____

What strategies do you use to resist peer pressure and stay true to yourself?

_____

_____

_____

_____

Do you think peer pressure has a bigger impact in middle school compared to elementary school? Why or why not?

_____

_____

_____

_____

How do you think peer pressure can influence decision-making and behavior in adolescence?

_____

_____

_____

_____

CULTIVATE POSITIVE THINKING

Positive thoughts create hopeful feelings and attract positive life experiences. A positive mind looks for ways a task can be done; a negative mind looks for ways it can't be done. Being positive doesn't mean that everything is good - it's changing your mindset to see the good in everything.

Hey Girl! Put your positive pants on; train your mind to see the good in everything. Positivity is a choice. The happiness of your life depends on the quality of your positive thoughts. When you focus on the good, the good increases. A great day that starts with a positive thought invites encouraging events throughout the day. Cultivating positive thinking is not about expecting the best to happen, rather it is about accepting that whatever happens is for the best.

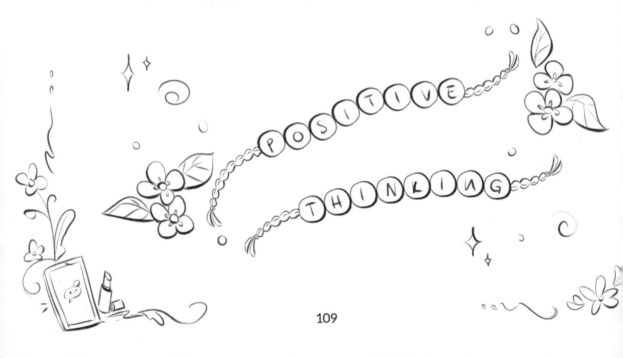

Positive Self-Talk

I felt good when...

I am proud of myself because...

I had fun when...

This makes me unique...

I like this about myself...

This was interesting today...

"Talk to yourself like you would to someone you love."

- Brené Brown

I learned from this mistake...

I love my....

I accomplished...

The best part of today was...

I feel strong when...

I am good at...

"Embrace your uniqueness. Time is much too short
to be living someone else's life." - Kobi Yamada

WORDS OF WISDOM

Needing support
is not a sign
of weakness

You don't have to be
an expert to start
a new adventure

Enforcing boundaries
doesn't make you
a bad person

You don't have to
get it right the first
time. Be open to learn

Focus on nurturing
your own life instead
of constantly
comparing it to others

You don't have to
feel brave to
be brave

25 THINGS YOU CAN CONTROL

Your thoughts

Your attitude

How honest you are

Your perspective

How often you exercise

Your beliefs

Who your friends are

What books you read

Whether or not you ask for help

The type of food you eat

How kind you are with yourself

The amount of effort you put forth

How you interpret situations

How you express your feelings

How you spend your money

How many times you smile today

How often you say "I love you"

How often you think about your past

How much time you spend worrying

How often you practice gratitude

How kind you are to others

Whether or not you judge other people

Whether or not you try again after a setback

How much you appreciate the things you have

How often you say "Thank you"

GROWTH MINDSET

Hey there, Awesome Girl!

A growth mindset is the belief that one's abilities and intelligence can be developed over time through effort, perseverance, and learning from mistakes. People with a growth mindset see challenges as opportunities for growth and view failure as a chance to learn and improve. This mindset fosters resilience, motivation, and a willingness to take on new challenges.

Imagine you're trying to learn how to ride a bike for the first time. At first, it might feel really hard, and you might fall off a few times. But if you have a growth mindset, you'll keep trying and practicing because you believe that you can get better with effort and time.

The same idea applies to dealing with puberty and body changes. When your body starts changing during puberty, it can feel confusing and sometimes uncomfortable. But having a growth mindset means believing that these changes are a normal part of growing up and that you can adapt and adjust to them.

For example, if you notice that you're getting taller or that your body shape is changing, instead of feeling worried or frustrated, you can think to yourself, "This is just my body growing and changing, and that's okay." You can also remind yourself that everyone goes through puberty at their own pace, and it's normal for bodies to change at different rates.

Having a growth mindset can also help you approach challenges related to puberty, like learning how to manage periods or dealing with acne, with a positive attitude. Instead of feeling discouraged if things don't go perfectly right away, you can see these challenges as opportunities to learn and grow.

Overall, a growth mindset helps you stay positive and resilient when dealing with puberty body changes and development by believing in your ability to adapt, learn, and grow through the process.

25 WAYS TO BUILD A GROWTH MINDSET

Practice Practice Practice

Exercise your brain. The more you use it, the stronger and smarter it becomes.

See challanges as opportunities to grow.

View failure as one step closer to your goals.

Ask questions when you don't understand something.

Seek self-compasion, not approval from others.

Look for ways to improve.

Work harder to get smarter.

Try a new path or strategy when one way is not working out.

Instead of saying, "I'm not good at this" ask "What am I missing?"

Set goals that are specific and doable.

Learn from mistakes

Use your creativity.

Remind yourself that you can do hard things.

Add "yet" to the end of "can't" sentences.

Accept and embrace your imperfections.

Avoid comparing yourself with others; instead learn from them.

Remember your intelligence is expandable.

Persist, keep working towards your goal even and especially when it's difficult.

Share what you're learning.

Focus on your effort, not on the result.

Believe that change is possible.

Think outside the box.

Use positive self-talk.

Don't give up until you're proud.

Color each box

116

ENJOY THE JOURNEY

Hey Girl! Don't wait for everything to be perfect. Accept and embrace where you are in your journey. Even if it's not where you want to be. There is a purpose to everything that happens in our lives. You don't have to know what comes next. You don't have to have everything figured out right this moment. You don't need to know your entire story.

You are a living, changing, growing soul, riding through your unique and beautiful journey of life. And that's exactly what it is— a journey— and it wouldn't be a journey if you knew everything that was coming next. It wouldn't be a journey if you knew how it would all turn out in the end. So be patient with yourself and smile at the unknown, because your story is just starting to be written.

What are some goals you have for yourself right now, and why are they important to you? _____
_____
_____

How do you prioritize your goals and decide which ones to focus on first? _____
_____
_____

Can you describe a time when you faced a challenge in reaching a goal? How did you handle it? _____
_____
_____
_____

What strategies do you use to stay focused and motivated when working towards a goal? _____

_____

_____

How do you deal with distractions or obstacles that may arise while pursuing your goals? _____

_____

_____

Do you find it helpful to break larger goals down into smaller, more manageable tasks? Why or why not? _____

_____

_____

How do you maintain a positive attitude and stay resilient in the face of setbacks or failures? _____

_____

_____

Do you set deadlines for yourself when working towards goals, or do you prefer to work at your own pace? Why?

_____

_____

Are there any role models or mentors who inspire you to set and achieve your goals? What qualities do they possess that you admire? _____

_____

_____

How do you celebrate your successes and milestones along the way to achieving your goals? _____

_____

_____

_____

12 habits of successful women

1. They always keep learning to keep moving forward.

2. They own their confidence in everything they do.

3. They set clear goals and go after them with determination.

4. They view setbacks as opportunities to grow.

5. They manage their time wisely to get things done efficiently.

6. They speak up confidently and without hesitation.

7. They build strong connections for support and growth.

8. They embrace change with strength and flexibility.

9. They take care of themselves as a top priority.

10. They lead with kindness and understanding.

11. They inspire others through their actions and words.

12. They are thankful for every experience and lesson they learn.

LOVE YOURSELF

Hey Girl! Hope you enjoyed going through this journal and found some value in my suggestions.

If you would like to get in touch with me, please email me PenMagicBooks@gmail.com

Much love and appreciation,
Pragya Tomar

GLOSSARY

Acne: Excess oil mixes with sweat and dirt, clogging pores and causing inflammation.

Areolae: Dark circles surrounding the nipples.

Blackheads: Excess oil mixes with sweat and dirt, clogging pores and darkening in color.

Breast bud: Hard bump beneath the nipple.

Caffeine: Ingredient in certain foods and drinks, potentially disrupting sleep.

Calcium: Mineral crucial for bone strength, deficiency leading to bone diseases.

Clitoris: Sensitive bud of skin atop the labia.

Consent: Permission required before engaging in any activity involving someone else's body.

Dandruff: Flakes of dead skin from the scalp.

Delayed puberty: Onset of puberty later than usual.

Dermatologist: Doctor specializing in skin care.

Discharge: Mucus and fluid resulting from increased hormones.

Estrogen: Hormone governing menstruation and other bodily functions.

Fallopian tubes: Tubes transporting eggs from ovaries to uterus.

Genitals: Private area.

Growing pains: Aches and pains in muscles, legs, and thighs accompanying growth spurts.

Growth spurt: Period of rapid growth involving arms, legs, feet, and hands.

Hormones: Chemicals facilitating changes during puberty.

Insomnia: Difficulty falling or staying asleep.

Labia: Inner and outer folds of skin on the vulva.

Meditation: Practice of sitting quietly to calm the mind.

Menopause: Cessation of menstruation in older women.

Menstruation: The shedding and release of blood and uterine lining from the vagina during a 28-day cycle.

Ova: Eggs stored in the ovaries.

Ovary: Sac-like organ producing and storing eggs, also releasing hormones to initiate puberty.

Ovulation: Release of an egg before menstruation.

Peer pressure: Influence from friends or classmates to do something against your wishes.

Precocious puberty: Early onset of puberty in girls.

Premenstrual syndrome (PMS): Symptoms experienced before menstruation, including tenderness, moodiness, bloating, and cramping.

Puberty: Stage of maturation enabling reproduction.

Pubic mound (mons pubis): Fleshy area below the belly.

Urethral opening/ Urethra: Hole below the clitoris for urine passage.

Uterus: Pear-shaped organ in the lower abdomen.

Vagina: Canal and opening leading to internal reproductive organs.

Vulva: External genital area.

Here are some useful websites for girls going through puberty:

KIDSHEALTH.org: Offers articles, quizzes, and videos covering various aspects of puberty in a kid-friendly format.

GIRLSHEALTH.gov: Provides information on puberty, body changes, and health topics specifically tailored for girls.

PLANNEDPARENTHOOD.org: Offers comprehensive information on sexual health, puberty, and reproductive rights for teens.

AMAZE.org: Provides animated videos and interactive resources on puberty, relationships, and sexual health education.

TEENSHEALTH.org: Offers articles, quizzes, and advice columns on puberty, emotions, and physical health for teenagers.

HELLOFLO.com: Offers articles and videos on puberty, periods, and body positivity, with a focus on empowering girls and young women.

GIRLSHELPINGGIRLSPERIOD.org
Offers comprehensive information on menstruation, serving as a supportive guide for beginners and provides insights on how to effectively use period products.

These websites offer reliable and age-appropriate information to help girls navigate the changes and challenges of puberty.

Made in United States
Troutdale, OR
08/28/2024

22403275R00071